P9-DWA-245

BOOKS BY JAMES MERRILL

Poetry

A SCATTERING OF SALTS   1995
SELECTED POEMS 1946–1985   1992
THE INNER ROOM   1988
LATE SETTINGS   1985
FROM THE FIRST NINE: POEMS 1946–1976   1982
THE CHANGING LIGHT AT SANDOVER   1982, 1992
SCRIPTS FOR THE PAGEANT   1980
MIRABELL: BOOKS OF NUMBER   1978
DIVINE COMEDIES   1976
BRAVING THE ELEMENTS   1972
THE FIRE SCREEN   1969
NIGHTS AND DAYS   1966
WATER STREET   1962
THE COUNTRY OF A THOUSAND YEARS OF PEACE   1959
(REVISED EDITION 1970)
FIRST POEMS   1951

Fiction

THE (DIBLOS) NOTEBOOK   1965, 1994
THE SERAGLIO   1957, 1987

Essays

RECITATIVE   1986

A Memoir

A DIFFERENT PERSON   1993

A Scattering of Salts

A Scattering of Salts

Poems by

James Merrill

Alfred A. Knopf   *New York*

1996

Copyright ©1995 by James Merrill

All rights reserved under International and Pan-American Copyright Conventions
Published in the United States by Alfred A. Knopf, Inc., New York, and simultane-
ously in Canada by Random House of Canada Limited, Toronto. Distributed by
Random House, Inc., New York.

Some of the poems originally appeared as follows:

Antaeus: Big Mirror Outdoors; A Look Askance; Scrapping the Computer
The Denver Quarterly: Volcanic Holiday
The Formalist: The Pyroxenes
Grand Street: Press Release
The Nation: Quatrains for Pegasus
The New Republic: A Downward Look
The New York Review of Books: Home Fires; Snow Job
The New Yorker: 164 East 72 Street; The "Ring" Cycle; Overdue Pilgrimage to Nova
    Scotia; Self-Portrait in Tyvek (TM) Windbreaker; Family Week at Oracle Ranch;
    Alabaster; The Great Emigration
The Paris Review: Two Novelettes; Tony: Ending the Life
Pequod: Pledge
Poetry: Nine Lives; Alessio and the Zinnias
Princeton University Library Chronicle: My Father's Irish Setters
The Southwest Review: Morning Exercise
U.S.C. Anthology: Rescue
Windhorse: Novelettes (3)
The Yale Review: The Ponchielli Complex; To the Reader; Cosmo

Nine Lives also appeared in a limited edition published by Nadja, with a drawing
by Dorothea Tanning, 1993.

Library of Congress Cataloging-in-Publication Data

Merrill, James Ingram.
    A scattering of salts : poems / by James Merrill.—1st ed.
        p.   cm.
    ISBN 0-679-44158-1
    I. Title.
PS3525.E6645S25   1995   94-42903
811'.54—dc20   CIP

Published March 29, 1995
Reprinted Five Times
Seventh Printing, February 1996

For Stephen Yenser

CONTENTS

Contents

I

A DOWNWARD LOOK

Seen from above, the sky
Is deep. Clouds float down there,

Foam on a long, luxurious bath.
Their shadows over limbs submerged in "air,"

Over protuberances, faults,
A delta thicket, glide. On high, the love

That drew the bath and scattered it with salts

Still radiates new projects old as day,
And hardly registers the tug

When, far beneath, a wrinkled, baby hand
Happens upon the plug.

BIG MIRROR OUTDOORS

Specter, inside with you where you belong!
Must the blond hibiscus be reminded
Of privileges tentatively won
From pay dirt? or our puppet selves grow pale
Here at their narrow lot's far end, beneath
Your glittering aplomb? Yes, yes, we know:
Artillery fern, chameleon, dinner guest,
Greens and blues, deck wreathed with fairy lights
Had begun, like us, to dodder and digress.
The realm of chance cried out for supervision.
One stroke, and the casino stood corrected—
A halfway house. Now yours, inviolate
Heart, is the last word, the cool view we shrink
To couple with. Yet breeding likenesses
That won't need food or shelter has become
(Given the hapless millions lured into
Our networks) an undertaking not entirely
Vain. Ah, even when it's death you deal—!
Puss lays the feathered fool at Uli's feet.
Too weak this year to set his easel up,
He'll render it in charcoal. Alone, later,
You will reflect the lighted pool while slowly,
Darkly in the pool revolves a float
On which two baby blots of dew reflect
Glimmerings of you. So that, much as the plot
Was to make do without us, sun and rain,
Reds and blacks, terrestrial roulette,
Nature grows strong in you. Again last night
Rustling forth in all her jewelry
She faced the glacial croupier: Double or nothing!
Again dawn hot and airtight found you sweating
Out that horrifying, harmless dream.

NINE LIVES

The ancient comic theater had it right:
A shuttered house, a street or square, a tree
Collect, life after life, the energy
To flood what happens in their shade with light.
A house in Athens does the trick for me—
Thrilling to find oneself again on stage,
In character, at this untender age.

I

[*Enters with DJ.*] . . . and the kitchen. Ours,
Along with all the rest. What are those headlines
Whose upper-case demotic holds the floor—
GET THE U. S. BASES OUT OF GREECE
—That old refrain, where's their imagination?
And what's outside?
                    [*A sullen, peeling door*
Wrenches open onto glare that weighs
So heavily on things, these August days
—And cats! The nursing mother stares appalled,
While one black kitten actually topples
Over in consternation before streaking
With three or four white siblings out of sight.]

That old shed houses them. The lilac shrub
Patient as a camel on its knees
Shades them. We used to water it—remember—
Magnanimously, with a warm, pulsing hose
From three flights up. Here in this basement flat
Lived old Miss Pesmazóglou and her cat,
Or cats. They seem to have made do without her.
Now we'll be on hand to mind them. Good of Gus
And Ab to rent the dear house back to us
While they're on tour. *You* take the upstairs. These
Half-buried rooms, so glimmeringly tiled—
The kittens also—keep me here, beguiled.

2

A dozen habits fostered by the scene
Spring back to life. Old troupers reemerge:
Tony and Nelly; from oblivion's verge
Strato himself, whose bloodshot eyes (once green)
And immense bulk confound the dramaturge.
There even comes an afternoon when, bored,
We sit down to a makeshift Ouija Board.

A courtesy call merely. No big deal.
A way of letting our familiars share
In these old haunts. Instead: U MUST PREPARE
YRSELVES. It's David's and my turn to keel
Over in consternation. YES MES CHERS
A CERTAIN 8 YEAR DARLING LEAVES BOMBAY
BY PLANE FOR ATHENS ONE WEEK FROM TODAY.

I hate to say it, but the neophyte
Must take the full amazement of this news
(At least till he can purchase and peruse
A heavy volume called *The Changing Light
At Sandover*) on faith.—What? Oh. My muse,
Smiling indulgently upon the wretch,
Authorizes a quick background sketch.

Maria Mitsotáki (here in Greece
An adored, black-clad mentor) crossed the bar,
From then on dazzling our binocular
Lenses, the poem's astral Beatrice,
Its very Plato. Now—OK so far?—
This bit of doctrine vital to our text:
Souls bright as hers quit one life for the next

Conscious, to what degree I shan't here tell,
Of where they lived and whom they used to know.
Maria was reborn eight years ago
In India, as a future (male) Nobel
Prize-winning chemist. The spring overflow
Of Ganges glittering with daybreak pales
Besides our wonder. CALL BACK FOR DETAILS

3

TREMORS MES CHERS SHAKE THE SUBCON [*The teacup*
Pauses, collects itself, glides on.] TINENT
AS THE CHATTERJEE FAMILY SERVANTS BUSILY PACK.
FATHER MADLY HINDU & MADLY PUNJABI
MEMBER OF PARLIAMENT, BANKER, FIREBRAND
COMING TO ATHENS AS A MEDIATOR
IN (HO HUM) GOVT TRADE TALKS. FAMILY
STAYING AT INDIAN EMBASSY INCLUDES
PAPPA, MAMMA & YOUNG SHANTIHPRASHAD
The magic child!
    [*Concerning whom we've gleaned*
Such tantalizing facts. For instance, he
Was spoken to at five by TINKLING VOICES
From test-tubes in his Junior Chemistry Kit.
At six turned WINE INTO WATER. *Lit at seven,*
While gardeners looked on goggle-eyed, HIS FIRST
SMOKELESS FIRE.]
     That tongue-twister's a name?
CALL HIM SHANTY: THIN, INTENSE BLACK EYES,
WEARING A FLAT STRAW HAT WITH LONG BLACK RIBBON
HE WILL NOT BE PARTED FROM. THAT IS YR CUE:
HAT BLOWS OFF (WITH OUR HELP IF NEED BE)
LANDING LATE AFTERNOON SEPTEMBER 4
NEAR (IF NOT ON) YR TABLE CAN U GUESS WHERE?

We can, of course. In Kolonáki Square,
At the Bon Goût, where we always met Maria.

TEATIME INDIAN FASHION MOTHER SLIM
IN PARIS CLOTHES, AYAH IN SARI. A LIMO
WILL WHISK THEM BACK TO PURDAH AFTER SHANTY
UTTERS THE SENTENCE HE HAS BEEN REHEARSING:
'WE WILL MEET AGAIN IN MY HOME CITY'

Well, it will be the proof we've never had
Or asked for. And if nothing happens, Ephraim?
If no hat sails our way? If D and I
Just wait like idiots? THE WIND WILL DIE

4

[*The following midday.*] David calls the cats
Our latest Holy Family. Why not?
Urania and hers have long outgrown
The Stonington arrangements. And indeed
A kind of "flight into Egypt" air pervades
The backdoor scene. Athens is full of Herods
Ready to massacre those innocents
Now suckling under leaves, now playing tag
On what to them must seem a parapet.
[*A three-foot drop divides our narrow "courtyard"*
From that of the house immediately downhill.]
Just after sunrise, watching as I set
The scraps out, which they're coming to depend on,
An old white tom, responsible and scarred—
Saint Joseph to the life—was standing guard.
He took no food; devoutly our eyes met.
The mother, too, with speaking glances said:
"Take him, my blackest and my wiliest,
Teach him the table manners of the West."
Later, the door left wide as usual,
A little bold black heart-shaped face peered in
To where I wrote, but fled my eager start.
If I could touch him—! Hasn't someone proven
That just to stroke a kitten, make it purr,

8

Lowers the blood pressure, both yours and its?
These kittens maddeningly don't concur:
The sight of me still throws them into fits.

[*With that, strides through the kitchen on the slender*
Chance that they're learning. Pandemonium.
The same black kitten somersaults—oh no!—
Backwards into the cement court below,
There taking refuge under an oil drum
Mounted on venerable two-by-fours
Complex and solid as the Trojan Horse.
No way to lure him out. In the other direction
A long escape route to the street leads past
The neighbors' house, promiscuously open
For renovations. Workmen come and go,
Plaster-white faces, joke and song. JM
Intends to play it cool in front of them.
Meanwhile for his—for everybody's sins
A frantic mewing back and forth begins.]

5

[*Two nights later.*] Talcum, loopy names
In an address book, strand of fine blond hair
Flossing a comb—God! if the Dutch au pair
Could sleep here . . . But my firework stratagems
To save the kitten fizzle in black air.
Today was Sunday. Not a soul next door.
The mother cat, cool on that canyon floor,

Suckled her black one. Ways to house and street
Were blocked, the hose hooked up. I hissed. He fled
To his old shelter. Quick! full stream ahead:
Faucet on, nozzle thumbed, a fluid sheet
Sliding beneath the oil-drum, out he sped,
Black lightning, eyes like headlights of a hit-and-run
Driver, the raison d'être of my kitten run!

With nimbleness approaching the sublime,
Seizing a bathtowel against fangs and claws
And lunging like an avatar of Shaw's
Life Force, I overtook my prey in time
To see him scuttle—not the slightest pause
Or pity for one instant laughingstock—
Into a vine-wreathed hole I'd failed to block.

The roof next door is level with our own.
It's there, as in a déjà-vu, mater-
ialized a mother dolefully—night was near—
Mewing down the drainpipe-telephone.
Feeling our eyes, "Now just see what you've done!"
Hers shone back. Such communicable pain!
From being human we grow inhumane.

We have, it seems, methodically wrecked
Her world. Analogies are rife and various
To worlds like Strato's, now disaster areas
We helped create. Hopeless to resurrect
Cradles of original neglect.
Our tidbits teach the kittens how to shit,
And day by day we put our foot in it.

6

[*Late evening, September 3.*] DJ:
Let's get some sleep. Tomorrow's the big day.

JM: All I can think about's my kitten.
It's sixty hours since we saw him last.
By now he's dying of thirst, wedged in the drainpipe . . .
I never should have opened that back door.

DJ: At least he has eight lives to go!
Remember when the Nestlé Company
Shipped its formula to Ghana, free?

The babies thrived on it. Then one fine morning,
End of shipments. No thought for all the mothers
Who weaned their babies on the formula
And had no milk left. There in a nutshell's
American policy.
                        JM: Say no more.
Leave every little skeleton in peace.
I never should have opened that back door.

7

[*Wednesday, 4 o'clock at the Bon Goût.*
Much harder to determine is the year.
Decades have passed since our first coffees here,
Ordered in dumbshow. Ah, if youth but knew!
The sky was then a sacramental blue,
The café's two old waiters dignified,
The tourist rare, nose buried in the Guide.]

DJ: There's a free table. It'll do . . .

[*Today's Bon Goût is more a minipark*
Cars eddy round. Yet here's a little breeze,
Respite of awnings, rustle of plane trees.
Real action won't begin till after dark.
Our glances wander—it's in fact a lark
Revisiting this former commonplace—
With guarded carelessness from face to face.]

DJ: The big thing is, they've all made money.
These young men don't have waistlines any more.
Do they still dance in pairs on the dirt floor?
JM: Would they still think our jokes were funny?

Nine Lives

[Sealed with red labels, wrapped in cellophane,
Aimed at some unsuspecting hostess, boom!
Off goes the florist's grand hydrangea bomb.
Green pinks, cream blues. Beneath its weight the vain
Eternal shopboy, scion of that swain
Who piped away the War of Independence,
Whistles egregiously for his descendants.]

Waiter: Caffé, Signori? Kein Problem.

[Living familiars infiltrate the scene.
The lottery man. Those two crème de la crème
Canasta-playing ladies. Trailing them,
The "Diplomat"?! Don't look, there's Fritz the Queen
From Chattanooga. But in olive-green
Cords and Chanel cloud a favorite Greek
Urbanely interrupts our hide-and-seek.]

Tony: Paidiá! In public? In the Square?
Mais c'est la fin du monde! I can't, I'm late—
I've found a buyer for that desk I hate.
Tomorrow noon, then? Nelly's cut her hair.

[Tomorrow noon we meet aboard the white
Boat to Spetsai, where a niece's villa
Is Nelly's all this month. The island's still a
Niche for the happy few. If they invite,
Who're we to be standoffish? Our first night
A widowed Gräfin hopes that we'll drop in
For camomile or cognac after din—]

DJ: A sari, look! JM: You're right—
No, look again. The company she's chosen
Disqualifies her—sideburns, Lederhosen . . .
Our ayah would be older, more soignée.
Besides, where's little Shanty? DJ [*sighing*]:
Delayed in traffic? Well, at least they're trying.

[*We look and look. Soon it's the absent faces*
We see. Mimí. Proud Chester. His evzone
"Of hollow bronze" from Thessaly. The crone—
Gray, toothless Papagena—hung with braces
Of snipe and quail. Called up from an oasis
Watered by Lethe, which no sun can warm,
They cower from our love like a sandstorm.]

JM: It's after five. My social graces
Are crumbling. Ten more minutes, would you say?

[*As shadows lengthen we prepare to pay,*
Collect ourselves, and bend our steps uphill.
Wait, though—how beautiful the light—sit still.
Now or never, as in the old play,
Its moonbeam-dappled feats performed by day,
Titania, Oberon, wake up! Employ
Your arts, produce that little Indian boy!

Long pause.] DJ: Well, let's be. On. Our. Way.

[*Giving the magic one last opportunity,*
Clutching at straws—if it should come to that,
We'd settle for a disembodied hat,
Flutter of black somewhere in the vicinity
To pin our hopes upon, if not our sanity—
We slowly get up. Eyes front. Dignified.
Two old ex-waiters. For the wind has died.]

8

[*Spetsai.*] The Gräfin: No, no, *I* am Greek,
My husband was a Hamburger. *He* spoke
The Ursprache. Oh later, perfect Greek,
But not our first year. I'm remembering—
Nelláki tells me you adored Maria—
Didn't we all—the party where Maria

And Helmut met for the first time. Without
A single word in common they communed.
They sat down on the sofa and *communed*
All evening long. Well, forty minutes. Thirty.
Quite long enough to make a bride of twenty
Run home in tears, and lock herself in the bathroom.
I'm ashamed *for* her to this day. I am!
Helmut was knocking, frantic. . . . All at once—
We lived those first years in "a wood near Athens"
As my grandfather liked to call Kifissia *then*—
No loud cafés, no traffic—all at once
Came music, music from nowhere, at one a.m.!
—Ah, don't ask me. Say the "Liebestraum"
Or something Viennese. But in this *dream*
Helmut and I met on the balcony. There
Below, like an Embarkment for Cythère,
Musicians from the party: clarinet,
Guitar, two violins. It must have been
Full moon, the garden seemed electrified,
And from the fiacre they'd come in—Maria
Waving the coachman's whip like a conductor.
We waved back, back in love. The summer night
Was young again. And then? She blew a kiss
And off they went clop-clop into the night.

Nelly [*back at the villa*]: Bah, che dream!
Moonlight and roses, pitiful old cat—
As if Maria's genre were operetta . . .

DJ: Come on, she's not so—cat? The *cat!*
I saw him—yes—this morning, our black kitten!
Meaning to tell you but it slipped my—where?
Down in the neighbors' court. No worse for wear.

9

MES CHERS WE OVERESTIMATED OURSELVES
Please don't apologize. If I may borrow
The Gräfin's genial phrase, we feel ashamed
For you already. FATHER CHATTERJEE
WD NOT ALLOW THEM OUT: SECURITY!
EMBASSY GUARDS HAD WARNED AGAINST THAT SQUARE
Innocent Kolonáki? I'll just bet.
YET (AND WE WEEP) OUR BRAVE BOY ROSE FROM HIS NAP
AS IF SLEEPWALKING & STOLE OUT UNSEEN
INTO THE STRANGE CITY. HE WAS FOUND
IN HIS PAJAMAS BY AN ANXIOUS CROWD.
'HELLO? HELLO? (IN ENGLISH, BUT SO FAINTLY)
WHERE ARE YOU?' HE WAS CALLING Ephraim, spare—
FORGIVE US. WE GREW OVERCONFIDENT.
A GRIEF FOR YOU, FAR GREATER FOR LITTLE SHANTY
SOBBING & FLAILING OUT JM DEAR SCRIBE
[*From whom burst certain long-pent-up reproaches
Ending:*] . . . the proof. The proof we've never had
Or, mind you, sought. Proof that you act in our theater
Not for once purely in a manner of speaking,
No: word made flesh. Flesh wailing, wide-eyed, seeking
Us! THE KITTEN LIVES! DJ'S PLAN SOUND
[*A stopgap ramp connecting the two levels.*]
I didn't mean the *kitten*— [*Here our revels
Grind to a halt on Ephraim's shifting ground.*]

Like Wise Men we'd been primed to kneel in awe
At journey's end before that child whose nature
Proved Earth at one with Heaven, and past with future.
Instead, the perfect fools we still are saw
A manger full of emptiness, dust, straw . . .
AND LIGHT! Well, yes. Light also. We weren't blind,
The sun was out. THE PLAY OF H E A V E N ' S M I N D

10

There is a moment comedies beget
When escapade and hubbub die away,
Vows are renewed, masks dropped, La Folle Journée
Arriving star by star at a septet.
It's then the connoisseur of your bouquet
(Who sits dry-eyed through *Oedipus* or *Lear*)
Will shed, O Happiness, a furtive tear.

We've propped the rough hypotenuse of board
Between the pit to which his fall consigned
Our prodigal and the haven left behind.
Nature must do the rest. No coaxing toward
The haggard matriarch on high. A blind
Protecting us, we smile down through the slats
As our flyblown road company of *Cats*

Concludes its run. (Did T. S. Eliot
Devise the whole show from his sepulcher?)
By dusk—black, white—the kittens suck and purr.
Shanty will fly, we're told, ON MIDNIGHT'S DOT
BACK TO HIS WASTE LAND—back, if you prefer,
To our subconscious, this much being sure:
That black hole is three-quarters literature.

(Why otherwise, midway in my fifth section,
Didn't I forestall my rhyme scheme's lapse,
Its walk downtown in sleep? Although, perhaps
Thanks to a nagging sense of misdirection
Once HEAVEN'S MIND came out from under wraps,
I've caught up with it, shaken it awake,
These aren't the "risks" a poem's meant to take.)

To all, sweet dreams. The teacup-stirring eddy
Is spent. We've dropped our masks, renewed our vows
To letters, to the lives that letters house,
Houses they shutter, streets they shade. Already
Empty and dark, this street is. Dusty boughs
Sleep in a pool of vigilance so bright
An old tom skirts it. The world's his tonight.

MORNING EXERCISE

Poem, neat pseudonym
For thoughts in disarray,
Tell how we'd gone that day
Separately to the gym.

I did things on a mat
To make me flexible.
The room was bare and chill;
I could relate to that.

You must have waded straight
Into the billowing steam,
Wanting to sweat your frame
Till choler stored of late

Should sparkle in your hair
And trickle down your chest.
So neither would have guessed
His missing half was there

Except that someone sane
(Between "my" room's and "yours"
Respective temperatures)
Had set a small, fogged pane

Through which—quick to bemuse
Wits for a change wiped clear—
Our eyes met. Oh my dear!
Against such interviews

Each pressed a sorry nose
And made his goldfish face:
Not much of an embrace
But better, I suppose,

For that. In ways a lot
Less fondly matter-of-fact
Might Eskimo enact
His bond with Hottentot. . . .

So be it. Dried and clad,
We took our homeward way,
Stopping for a parfait
Aux fraises at the Old Grad.

ALABASTER

1
The original word
Eddied and forked, to mean (a) the soft stone
In use today—flamboyant, vaguely lewd
Honey-pink volumes flounced with lard
Like Parma ham, like the blown-up
Varnished nipple of a Titian nude.

Then (b) the ancient one—
A kind of Pharaonate of Lime,
Cosmetic white, or unbleached-linen white
Through which waves cresting purer white
Make a river seem to stand upright
When the jar fills with sun.

You could say that vagabond gypsum and sacerdotal
Calcite embody the two
Mainstreams of Western thought—Aristotle
And Plato, gristle and dream;
Also that on those mornings they're shone through
Both are supreme.

2
Thanks to it, for centuries a glow
Not quite of this world lit
Sanctum, princeling, folio.
Always too late
We saw the stricken cow, the rabble below
With catapult and crossbow.

Now came the age of glass.
Each room boasted a device whereby
Misbehavior, even miles away,
Could be perceived. (Uh-oh.
From then on it was curtains, both for us
And for the window.)

Visible meanwhile, we had to clean
Our act up. Probity, good sense?
Zero to 1 on the Mohs scale—yet, we'd learn,
Indistinguishable on a wide screen
From marble, rosy with concern:
The stuff of Presidents.

3
And if a tissue-thin
Section of self lay on a lighted slide,
And a voice breathed in your ear,
"Yes, ah yes. That red oxide
Stain is where your iron, Lady Hera,
Entered him.

And in this corner, boldly intricate
As agate, zigzagging
Bays and salients—plans of a fortress?—date
From his twentieth spring,
When we had set the dials at *First Love*.
Up here's the opalescent fossil of—"

Dream on. Dodo and roc
Did without your pious autopsies.
Nor will the self resist,
Broken on terror like a rack,
When waves of nightmare heat decrystallize
Her lucid molecules to chalk.

4
Landscapes about to disappear
Absorb what life
They can. Tamped rainbows tallied
The eons of one banded cliff.
Time pressing hawk and asp and onager
Each to its hieroglyph,

Alabaster

Gods fled to high ground. The dam totally
Quashed—like a warlord—
The future of that past. Henceforward
As text and text alone would the sacred valley
Invite construction. Shall we
Go to the blackboard?

October Flood Sun Set
[The] *Water Table Rising Presences*
[Balance the] *Mirror* [upon] *Granite Knees*
[A] *Scorpion* [made of] *Gems* [in it]
—The so-called "zodiac" cartouche of Sut
Found (1904) by Côme de Guise.

5
In Spring but also now in Fall
Earth's tilt allows
Early sun to flow straight through the house,
So catching a catch-all
Thrift-shop table in the upstairs hall
That its translucent inset glows,

Mild, otherworldly, from the underside.
As once in love or infancy
Yesterday's cargo—pine cone, junk mail, key—
Floats on a milky tide,
Grime-swirled, with blood-pink glimmerings. For me
The time I dread

Is coming, thinks the table. Yet despite
All that, these fine, late days,
Long minutes after dawn, whatever weighs
Upon me light
Bears up, as to recall it does
Through the dry channel of a starless night.

SNOW JOBS

X had the funds, the friends, the plan.
Y's frank grin was—our common fate?
Or just a flash in just a pan?
Z, from the tender age of eight,
Had thirsted to officiate.
We hardly felt them disappear,
The crooked and the somewhat straight.
Now where's the slush of yesteryear?

Where's Teapot Dome? Where's the Iran
Contra Affair? Where's Watergate—
Liddy—Magruder—Erlichman?
Their shoes squeaked down the Halls of State,
Whole networks groaned beneath their weight,
Till spinster Clotho darted near
To shroud in white a running mate.
Ah, where's the slush of yesteryear?

Like blizzards on a screen the scan-
dals thickened at a fearful rate,
Followed by laughter from a can
And hot air from the candidate.
With so much open to debate,
Language that went into one ear
Came out the—hush! be delicate:
Where is the slush of yesteryear?

Omniscient Host, throughout your great
Late shows the crystal wits cohere,
The flaky banks accumulate—
But where's the slush of yesteryear?

HOME FIRES

for John Hollander

I peered into the crater's heaving red
And quailed. I called upon the Muse. I said,
   "The day I cease to serve you, let me die!"
And woke alone to birdsong, in our bed.

The flame was sinewed like those angels Blake
Drew faithfully. One old log, flake by flake,
   Gasped out its being. Had it hoped to rise
Intact from such a wrestler's give-and-take?

My house is made of wood so old, so dry
From years beneath this pilot-light blue sky,
   A stranger's idle glance could be the match
That sends us all to blazes.—Where was I?

Ah yes. The man from Aetna showed concern.
No alarm system—when would people learn?
   No outside stair. The work begins next week.
Must I now marry that I may not burn?

Never again, oracular, wild-eyed,
To breathe on a live ember deep inside?
   The contract signed in blood forbids that, too,
Damping my spirit as it saves my hide.

Take risks! the crowd chants in a kind of rage
To where his roaring garret frames the sage
   Held back by logic, by the very thought
Of leaping to conclusions, at his age.

Besides, the cramped flue of each stanza draws
Feeling *away*. To spare us? Or because
   Heaven is cold and needs the mortal stuff
Flung nightly around its barenesses, like gauze.

Last weekend in a bar in Pawcatuck
A boy's face raw and lean as lightning struck.
  Before I knew what hit me, there you were,
Sweetheart, with your wet blanket. Just my luck.

I touched the grate with my small hand, and got
Corrected. Sister ran to kiss the spot.
  Today a blister full of speechless woe
Wells up for the burnt children I am not.

Magda was molten at sixteen. The old
Foundryman took his time, prepared the mold,
  Then poured. Lost wax, the last of many tears,
Slid down her face. Adieu, rosebuds and gold!

That slim bronze figure of Free Speech among
Repressive glooms woke ardor in the young,
  Only to ring with mirth—a trope in Czech
Twisting implacably the fire's tongue.

One grace: this dull asbestos halo meant
For the bulb's burning brow. Two drops of scent
  Upon it, and our booklined rooms, come dusk,
Of a far-shining lamp grew redolent.

The riot had been "foretold" to Mrs Platt,
The landlady, by a glass ruby at
  The medium's throat. "Next she'll be throwing fits,"
Gerald said coldly. "I shall move. That's that."

Torchlit, the student demonstrators came.
Faint blues and violets within the flame
  Appeared to plead that fire at heart was shy
And only incidentally to blame.

Consuming fear, that winter, swept the mind.
Then silence, country sounds—and look! Behind
   Me stands the blackened chimney of our school,
Crowned with a stork's nest, rambler-rose-entwined.

A sunset to end all. Life's brave disguise—
Rages and fevers, worn to tantalize—
   Flickers to ash. What's left may warm itself
At the hearth glowing in its lover's eyes.

★

Dear Fulmia, I thought of you for these
Obsidian trinkets purchased, if you please,
   In a boutique at the volcano's core.
(Extinct? I wonder.) Love, Empedocles.

THE *RING* CYCLE

I

They're doing a *Ring* cycle at the Met,
Four operas in one week, for the first time
Since 1939. I went to that one.
Then war broke out, Flagstad flew home, tastes veered
To tuneful deaths and dudgeons. Next to Verdi,
Whose riddles I could whistle but not solve,
Wagner had been significance itself,
Great golden lengths of it, stitched with motifs,
A music in whose folds the mind, at twelve,
Came to its senses: Twin, Sword, Forest Bird,
Envy, Redemption through Love. . . . But left unheard
These fifty years? A fire of answered prayers
Burned round that little pitcher with big ears
Who now wakes. Night. E-flat denotes the Rhine,
Where everything began. The world's life. Mine.

2

Young love, moon-flooded hut, and the act ends.
House lights. The matron on my left exclaims.
We gasp and kiss. Our mothers were best friends.
Now, old as mothers, here we sit. Too weird.
That man across the aisle, with lambswool beard,
Was once my classmate, or a year behind me.
Alone, in black, in front of him, Maxine. . . .
It's like the *Our Town* cemetery scene!
We have long evenings to absorb together
Before the world ends: once familiar faces
Transfigured by hi-tech rainbow and mist,
Fireball and thunderhead. Make-believe weather
Calling no less for prudence. At our stage
When recognition strikes, who can afford
The strain it places on the old switchboard?

3

Fricka looks pleased with her new hairdresser.
Brünnhilde (Behrens) has abandoned hers.
Russet-maned, eager for battle, she butts her father
Like a playful pony. They've all grown, these powers,
So young, so human. So exploitable.
The very industries whose "major funding"
Underwrote the production continue to plunder
The planet's wealth. Erda, her cobwebs beaded
With years of seeping waste, subsides unheeded
—Right, Mr President? Right, Texaco?—
Into a gas-blue cleft. Singers retire,
Yes, but take pupils. Not these powers, no, no.
What corporation Wotan, trained by them,
Returns gold to the disaffected river,
Or preatomic sanctity to fire?

4

Brünnhilde confronts Siegfried. That is to say,
Two singers have been patiently rehearsed
So that their tones and attitudes convey
Outrage and injured innocence. But first
Two youngsters became singers, strove to master
Every nuance of innocence and outrage
Even in the bosom of their stolid
Middleclass families who made it possible
To study voice, and languages, take lessons
In how the woman loves, the hero dies. . . .
Tonight again, each note a blade reforged,
The dire oath ready in their blood is sworn.
Two world-class egos, painted, overweight,
Who'll joke at supper side by side, now hate
So plausibly that one old stagehand cries.

5

I've worn my rings—all three of them
At once for the first time—to the *Ring*.

Like pearls in seawater they gleam,
A facet sparkles through waves of sound.

Of their three givers one is underground,
One far off, one here listening.

One ring is gold; one silver, set
With two small diamonds; the third, bone
—Conch shell, rather. Ocean cradled it

As earth did the gems and metals. All unknown,
Then, were the sweatshops of Nibelheim

That worry Nature into jewelry,
Orbits of power, Love's over me,

Or music's, as his own chromatic scales
Beset the dragon, over Time.

6

Back when the old house was being leveled
And this one built, I made a contribution.
Accordingly, a seat that bears my name
Year after year between its thin, squared shoulders
(Where Hagen is about to aim his spear)
Bides its time in instrumental gloom.
These evenings we're safe. Our seats belong
To Walter J. and Ortrud Fogelsong
—Whoever they are, or were. But late one night
(How is it possible? I'm sound asleep!)
I stumble on "my" darkened place. The plaque
Gives off that phosphorescent sheen of Earth's
Address book. Stranger yet, as I sink back,
The youth behind me, daybreak in his eyes—
A son till now undreamed of—makes to rise.

THE PONCHIELLI COMPLEX

"Suicidio!"

Husbands, by my time, dozed beneath the gilt.
The Golden Age was ending, that began
With ominous panache. It was the man
Back then who, lighthouse-monocle aflash
From the deep, twilit loge, willed Malibran
To go insane and ripplingly expire.

He or the likes of him had tamed the wild
Horses of steam, made fiction of the trees.
Soon cables would floor Ocean, factories
Sweat dusk at noon, dehydrating the child
Lighter and bleaker than a lump of coal.
Already Nature, footlit in the guise
Of a wronged maiden, (did he realize?)
Expressed what this was doing to the soul.

A woman who had spent her youth at scales
Until hers glinted undertook the role.
Given her life—alone and badly paid—
She needed a protector. That old score
Had ups and downs aplenty, which she played
Also to the hilt. His noisy shirt.
His wife. His friends who treated her like dirt.

Each latest outburst caused increasingly
Fine sunsets round the world. Just so, the sweet
Unsullied heroines of her first decade
Were changing. Now consumptive milliners,
Demi-mondaines and fat Venetian street
Singers driven to verismo's brink
Got their deserts. I poured a triple drink

And wrote: *The end. No more roulades.* But then
Our high seas quieted and the sun shone.
What would acting on that mood have meant?
Strangling the lamia whose decibels
Were slowly turning the proscenium
Muses to plaster? Or bankrupting him,
Yearly stouter and more somnolent,
Who backed whatever war-horse she starred in?

Neither. It would have meant once and for all
Extinguishing the footlights across which
Their glances met: desire, intelligence,
Asperity, ennui . . . —per carità!
Not with her clutch-and-stagger scene beginning,
That brings the house down and him backstage grinning.

TO THE READER

Each day, hot off the press from Moon & Son,
"Knowing of your continued interest,"
Here's a new book—well, actually the updated
Edition of their one all-time best seller—
To find last night's place in, and forge ahead.
If certain scenes and situations ("work,"
As the jacket has it, "of a blazingly
Original voice") make you look up from your page
—*But this is life, is truth, is me!*—too many
Smack of self-plagiarism. Terror and tryst,
Vow and verbena, done before, to death,
In earlier chapters, under different names . . .
And what about *those* characters? No true
Creator would just let them fade from view
Or be snuffed out, like people. Yet is there room
(In the pinch of pages under your right thumb)
To bring them back so late into their own?—
Granted their own can tell itself from yours.
You'd like to think a structure will emerge,
If only a kind of Joycean squirrel run
Returning us all neatly to page 1,
But the inconsistencies of plot and style
Lead you to fear that, for this author, fiction
Aims at the cheap effect, "stranger than fiction,"
As people once thought life—no, *truth* was. Strange . . .
Anyhow, your final thought tonight,
Before you kiss my picture and turn the light out,
Is of a more exemplary life begun
Tomorrow, truer, harder to get right.

VOLCANIC HOLIDAY

I
Our helicopter shaking like a fist
Hovers above the churning
Cauldron of red lead in what a passion!
None but the junior cherubim ask why.
We bank and bolt. Shores draped in gloom
Upglint to future shocks of wheat.
Your lips, unheard, move through the din of blades.

2
A Mormon merman, God's least lobbyist,
Prowls the hotel. All morning
Sun tries to reason with the mad old ocean
We deep down feel the pull of. And in high
Valleys remote from salt and spume
Waterfalls jubilantly fleet
Spirit that thunder into glancing braids.

3
Thunder or bamboos drumming in the mist?
Tumbril or tribal warning?
Pacific Warfare reads the explanation
For a display we'd normally pass by:
Molars of men who snarled at doom
Studding a lava bowl. What meat
Mollifies the howl of famished shades?

4
Crested like palms, like waves, they too subsist
On one idea—returning.
Generation after generation
The spirit grapples, tattered butterfly,
A flower in sexual costume,
Hardon or sheath dew-fired. Our feet
At noon seek paths the evening rain degrades.

5

Adolescence, glowering unkissed:
The obstacle course yearning
Grew strong in. Cheek to cliff face, sheer devotion. . . .
To be loved back, then, would have been to die.
Then, not now. Show me the tomb
Whose motto and stone lyre compete
With this life-giving fever. As it fades

6

From the Zen chapel comes that song by Liszt.
Is love a dream? A burning,
Then a tempering? Beyond slopes gone ashen,
Rifts that breathe gas, rivers that vitrify,
Look! a bough falters into bloom.
Twin rainbows come and go, discreet,
As when together we haunt virgin glades.

7

Moments or years hence, having reminisced,
May somebody discerning
Arrive at tranquil words for . . . mere emotion?
Meanwhile let green-to-midnight shifts of sky
Fill sliding mirrors in our room
—No more eruptions, they entreat—
With Earth's repose and Heaven's masquerades.

RESCUE

Dusk. Rain over   but asphalt hissing
flooded clear   with sea light.
Sharply, sweet heart,   you swerved, pulled off,
ran back and snatching   the three-inch turtle
we almost hadn't   missed as it started
its perilous crossing   deposited it
there! at the far   pasture's edge—
mission so nimbly,   raptly accomplished
where dizzying beams   rushed both ways
and tears broke   from the tall trees
that I who saw   the marvel simply
filed it away   for future use.
We'd seen so many   marvels those days:

Water welling   from a mountain top.
The Fire goddess   faithfully bleeding
into the Sea,   our helicopter's
crawling shadow   a fly on folds of
charcoal lamé.   From higher yet,
eye to eye   with the ever grander
rising Sun,   the full Moon setting.
Our own two bodies   burnished by foam
—ah, and Rainbows   appearing in pairs
(the showy male,   his mate shyer,
like a Japanese   bride and groom)
peaceably browsing   on the jacaranda
grove in palest   purple bloom.

Back to the turtle,   here's a tale
it can tell   till the end of time:
"Night was falling.   Too frightened to shrink
into my shell,   as the shattering lights
hurtled past   I took despairingly
slow steps   to appease them.
Upon chelonian   powers that shouldered
Terra herself   from a waste of waters

childlike I called   for help. Was heard!—
only then turning   to instinctive stone.
Shame upon me: I had shut myself to
life even   as it uplifted
and heaved me into   a green haven."

II

THE INSTILLING

All day from high within the skull—
Dome of a Pantheon, trepanned—light shines
Into the body. Down that stair

Sometimes there's fog: opaque red droplets check
The beam. Sometimes tall redwood-tendoned glades
Come and go, whose dwellers came and went.
Now darting feverishly anywhere,
Manic duncecap its danseuse eludes,

Now slowed by grief, white-lipped,
Grasping the newel bone of its descent,

This light can even be invisible

Till a deep sparkle, regular as script,
As wavelets of an EKG, defines
The dreamless gulf between two shoulder blades.

NOVELETTES

I

We have settled into this resort hotel.
Our blue suite, linked to others, overlooks a lake's
Cloudless reflections. People we more or less know
Make up the clientele. Next door, for instance,
Two little girls of six, one fair, one dark
(Summer and Winter you called them) are at play—
Hear their shrieks of laughter . . . of pain? *Of pleasure!*
The children, obscenely compliant, are being tortured
By white men dressed in black. You race for the sauna
To fetch their mother from the blinding steam.
She comes forth dripping, red as fire. What next
Happens happens in a flash. Our entire wing
(In conformance to some prevailing "binary plan")
Is now a museum: walls, tables, floor to ceiling
Dense with memorabilia—wrenches, fingernails,
Theater stubs, half-done needlework. Or rather
Not these but laser projections of the lost originals.
I move, on my cane, through crowds; it's the last day.
Concerning one exhibit, a young Eurasian
With a press card stops me: "Sir, can you tell our viewers
How much, in those old plays of yours, were the actors paid?"
Rough figures come to mind. "So little? That's
What you called a living?" Still bent on finding you,
I hobble past. Here's a window onto a world of moonlit
Cubes and arches in ruins, populated by cats.

2

A mesa at cloud level. Over the side, tucked far,
Far down in emerald crevices, appear
Signs of civilization. The descent is sheer,
Yet sturdy dappled ponies have been bred
For just this purpose. We dismount—we three—
To an enchantment of cobbled streets and foggy
Lantern-lit shops: an English town. From the speech,
The bonnets and coins, the cakes and tortoiseshell,
Lamia & Other Poems (three mint copies)
We deduce that nothing has changed since 1820.
We take rooms. Time stands still—and flies. Each day
New charms emerge. People are reticent
But ready, we feel, to accept us. So much so
That the blow stuns, when it falls. Two officers
Materialize interrogating J
Who counters, with reason, that we've shown good faith,
Asked from the start no better than to stay.
"Ah," says the tall one in a more civil tone,
Ushering us past gawking groom and barmaid
Out of the inn, "'tis so, you three well-nigh . . .
But here are your horses." The ascent is harrowing
Into the faceless glare and windhowl. In its course
A fan of stiffened gauze—our only proof,
M will keep laughing later, fighting back tears—
Falls from her sash, through cloud-shreds, past retrieval.

3

The house has filled and darkened. *The Magic Flute*
Begins in silence. A gang of urchins
Racked like pool balls as the curtain parts
Break through the audience, spraying the faces
Of a startled few with luminous paint. A chill
Quick-drying coat transfigures mine. Thus chosen,
We're herded—old subscribers left behind
Blinking about in confusion—onto the stage.
It brightens. We must not look back. The theater
Has no back. In twos (our guides older by now,
More reticent—yet some first true chord is struck)
We have an endless pier of planks to walk, a white
Ramshackle xylophone set low above the flats.
All is tranquillity. To soaring strings
The gradual wavelets glitter, their bluegreen deepens
—But my friend? He's fallen (did the staves give way?)
Head downward, sinking like a stone. I jump in after,
If only to—but there he goes, borne past me
Limp in the jaws of a great fire-gilled sunfish!
A line I've made him grasp will haul him back
To air, the dominant. Except that now *I'm* lost
Beneath the surface, among these milkily glinting
Minors, these time-colored motes, precipitate
Of music, from which I must be saved. I hear him
Piping, trying to reach me. And wake unafraid. He will.

MY FATHER'S IRISH SETTERS

Always throughout his life
(The parts of it I knew)
Two or three would be racing
Up stairs and down hallways,
Whining to take us walking,
Or caked with dirt, resigning
Keen ears to bouts of talk—
Until his third, last wife
Put down her little foot.
That splendid, thoroughbred
Lineage was penned
Safely out of earshot:
Fed, of course, and watered,
But never let out to run.
"Dear God," the new wife simpered,
Tossing her little head,
"Suppose they got run over—
Wouldn't *that* be the end?"

Each time I visited
(Once or twice a year)
I'd slip out, giving my word
Not to get carried away.
At the dogs' first sight of me
Far off—of anyone—
Began a joyous barking,
A russet-and-rapid-as-flame
Leaping, then whimpering lickings
Of face and hands through wire.
Like fire, like fountains leaping
With love and loyalty,
Put, were they, in safekeeping
By love, or for love's sake?
Dear heart, to love's own shame.
But loyalty transferred
Leaves famously slim pickings,
And no one's left to blame.

My Father's Irish Setters

Divorced again, my father
(Hair white, face deeply scored)
Looked round and heaved a sigh.
The setters were nowhere.
Fleet muzzle, soulful eye
Dead lo! these forty winters?
Not so. Tonight in perfect
Lamplit stillness begin
With updraft from the worksheet,
Leaping and tongues, far-shining
Hearths of our hinterland:
Dour chieftain, maiden pining
Away for that lost music,
Her harpist's wild red hair. . . .
Dear clan of Ginger and Finn,
As I go through your motions
(As they go through me, rather)
Love follows, pen in hand.

THE GREAT EMIGRATION

On the low road to Skye
Many a scenic detour,
Oddly few people—
Who's to say why?

THE GLEN. They were my brave lads and I failed them. Failed
to believe their oaths, sworn in my very bosom. To grasp how that
matter of a royal line kept leading not to the stanza where weapons
glanced peaceably from walls of Spanish leather, but to the battle-
field. Small wonder my flowers of manhood sprang up blood-red in
clearings of a far, uncharted land. Yonder would follow them no
agent of the Crown.

More braes, more lochs . . .
Ever fewer bipeds. Ghosts of rain,
A West grown tame and woolly,
Flocked by flocks

—Sheep or stones? Scrambling to their feet
As we whiz by
A local rock group
Begins to bleat.

Yet where cloud-rents
Brighten up ahead
The scene gives back its promptest gleam so far
Of intelligence.

THE LOCH. Don't be fooled. Man-shaped at first, distended
now by spasms old as the hills to this stretch-mark of twilight upon
barren green, my mind is failing something wonderful. No more
ideas, no more fair faces quizzing me. It's gust and peak from now
on, it's brute beak of swan. I seem abstracted? Don't be fooled.
When no one's looking the Thing surfaces.

Wrinkled and barnacled—each a whale
Shaped by unplumbable pressures—
Stone after standing stone
Breaches into the gale.

And the sunlit moon, strange as the moor we cross
Toward a meal featuring
"Medallions of peat
Smothered in rich cream sauce" . . .

THE HAG. I go on. And on. Brick by brick, the same old story. In the palsied hovels it comes to light—comes rather to eye-watering reek. Dogged as Auld MacAdam cutting into my squelchy terrine, the new crust forms. Brick by brick—but there I go, repeating myself. And no one listens anymore.

Those crags, at noon so threatening to approach,
Midnight wears on her bosom
Backed by expiring day,
An onyx brooch.

BEN NEVIS. With the sailing of the first ships such a grief shook us. Folk left behind fell onto the shore weeping like children. Another year and the grievers, too, set sail—hear their skirling in the skua's throat? Naught remains but to rise in lonely mist above my old, contrary fault. For I too had defected; had by slow unwitting eastward millimeters broken faith with titans whose bones today, ground fine as sugar, seal up the Fountain of Youth.

Sunrise. "The Sands of Uig"—
Quaverings by Schumann
Of a transparence
Marked *sanft und ruhig.*

THE MONSTER. They have diagnosed my presence, never found me. A shape-shifter, I mutate, I metastasize. Hairshirt tweeds from the gaunt weavers of Bigotree. The broken vow, the cell's implosion. A dread my hostess dissembles with cloudlets, rippling puns, the carnival mask of the swan. But [*a whisper*] beneath that silver evening gown she's wasting away.

Should the rainbow fret,
Each color in its parched enamel cot,
Deftly, inspiredly
Like a healer, your wet

Brush makes the rounds. And presently, mixing *their*
Mothers-of-pearl and pale
Kelp-scribbled creams,
The little coves bid fair

To last. Heaven's eye
Sparkles from the crater of one huge
Lava-purple cowflop, marking a path
Wisps of white prettify:

"Lamb's wool in ears
Before our dip, love!"—Nanny's voice.
Thirty degrees of latitude away
And twice that many years

Welcome palm, plumbago, joy
Of the live deep sapphire
Key-studded Stream
I swam in as a boy—

THE NORTH ATLANTIC. You caught my Drift! Aye, aye, I love you still. Who else contrived this rendezvous with mildness, here at journey's end? Subtly reversing the trend from youth to age, from Key to Loch, from New World to Old Country, I am the quittance you sought. Pray do not thank me. The trouble is lost in the pleasure.

Pleasure? Or just Geography cloud-swirled
With Time, a moonwalk's black-and-blue
Postage stamp of Earth . . . Well,
News from a far corner of the world,

Our only envelope. But what to say
Inside, and who to mail it to?
"Great Hermes, Psychopomp,
We're all packed. Lead the way . . ."

T H E   S W A N.   Would ye hear my song? Tune in another morning.

The postmistress in her fluorescent hole
Weighs (before cancelling) this latest
History of slow-motion joys and grievances
Under remote control.

MORE OR LESS

Nature copies Art, said Oscar Wilde.
Out therefore with the old inheritance,
Rooms so overfurnished the heart sinks,
Moulding and fringe, high ozone-whitened panes,
Precious woods and mirror cataract,
The million doodad species catching dust.
In with lack of clutter, starkly styled,
Only the fittest vertebrates and plants,
Cactus habitat and goldfish bowl,
Little to smarten up our costly prefab
Unless a holograph of (say) Einstein—
Bespectacled, white-maned, a breathing sphinx—
Prints ever-thinning air with the myopic
Simplicity of those who live here still,
Their sad knowhow, their fingertip control.

ON THE BLOCK

1   *Lamp, Terracotta Base, U.S, ca. 1925*

If when you're old and musing
Upon my whats and whys
Another one should flicker
Its last before your eyes

Don't worry, they give out, too,
Those burning filaments,
Imagination's debris
Englobed still in a sense

Briefly too hot to handle,
Too dim a souvenir,
Then, for the deft unscrewing
Unless you first, my dear,

Feel for what it shone from,
Ribbed clay each night anew
Hardened to its mission:
Light for the likes of you.

2   *Mantel Clock, Imitation Sèvres*

Time, passing, glances at the clock
Perhaps with pity—who's to say?
Still rose and ormolu, its hands
Clasped in dismay . . .

"Stay then, thou art so fair," he smiles,
To put the pretty thing at ease.
"I will, *I have*," the latter sighs.
"Now what, please?

Teach me to tick without the touch
I took my life from—ah, those years!"
It's dusk; the dial brims with faint
Firefly tears.

The arbiter reviews a face
Flawless in its partial knowing:
"Child, think well of me, or try.
I must be going."

SCRAPPING THE COMPUTER

Like countless others in the digital age, I seem
To have written a memoir on my new computer.
It had no memories—anyone's would have done,
And mine, I hoped, were as good as anyone's.
This playmate was programmed for my "personal" needs,
(A bit too intricately, it would transpire)
But all was advancing at the smooth pace of dream

Until that morning when a faint mechanical shriek
Took me aback. As I watched, the paragraph
Then under way deconstructed itself into
Mathematical symbols, musical notation—
Ophelia's mad scene in a Czech production
Fifty years hence. The patient left on a gurney,
Returned with a new chip, the following week.

Another year or two, the memoir done
And in the publishers' hands, the pressure's off.
But when I next switch it on, whatever Descartes meant
By the ghost in the machine—oh damn!—gives itself up:
Experts declare BRAIN DEATH. (The contriver of my program
Having lately developed a multiple personality,
My calls for help kept reaching the wrong one.)

Had it caught some "computer virus"? For months now a post-
Partum depression holds me prisoner:
Days spent prone, staring at the ceiling,
Or with an arm flung over my eyes. Then sleepless nights
In which surely not *my* fingertips upon the mattress
Count out Bach, Offenbach, Sousa, trying to fit
Into groups of five or ten their metronomanic host.

Or was the poor thing taking upon itself a doom
Headed my way? Having by now a self of sorts,
Was it capable of a selfless act
As I might just still be, for someone I loved?
Not that a machine is capable of anything *but*
A selfless act. . . . We faced each other wordlessly,
Two blank minds, two screens aglow with gloom.

Or perhaps this alter ego'd been under "contract"—*Yep,*
You know too much, wise guy. . . . Feet in cement,
A sendoff choreographed by the Mob.
But who the Mob is, will I ever know?
—Short of the trillionfold synaptic flow
Surrounding, making every circumstance
Sparkle like mica with my every step

Into—can that be sunlight? Ah, it shines
On women in furs, or dreadlock heads on knees,
(Hand-lettered placards: BROKE. ILL. HELP ME PLEASE),
This prisoner expelled to the Free World,
His dossier shredded. Now for new memories,
New needs. And while we're at it a novice laptop
On which already he's composed these lines.

A LOOK ASKANCE

Skyward mazes
Rise at right angles to a downstream
Current (left), eluding the pedestrian

Only at the steep cost of fixed scope
And enforced togetherness. Head tilted
In appraisal, see how their concrete poem

Keeps towering higher and higher. See also at dusk
Meaning's quick lineman climb from floor to floor
Inlaying gloom with beads of hot red ore

That hiss in the ferry's backwash, already
Turning to steam where strobe-lit X trains quake
For the commuters of our day

To night. And tomorrow when muggy noon
Films the slow float of peacenik or militant deviate
Down who'll be left to say which of the straight

White avenues between these tercets, when the confetti
Punctuation, the tickertape neologisms begin to pour
From the mad speed-writer plugged into the topmost outlet,

Will it be heat of his—our—bright idea
Makes that whole citywide brainstorm incandesce,
Sets loop, dot, dash, node, filament

Inside the vast gray-frosted bulb ablaze?—
The fire-fonts, the ash script descending
Through final drafts of a sentence

Passed upon us even as we pass into this
Fossil state thought up, then idly
Jotted down on stone.

PRESS RELEASE

Now comes word that a new synthetic substance
Crystallized in Sacramento for the first time.
After much coaxing. These virgin substances
Don't know how. Or it "hurts" like the first time
You were kissed by a man. From then on, each time
Gets easier and perhaps—with crystals, who knows?—
More pleasurable. So now this enlightened substance,
Its code (so to speak) cracked, its maidenhead taken,
Unblinkingly reenacts, time after time,

And in remote labs, a rite of passage unknown
Two weeks ago. Will someone please undertake
To say how the leak occurred? As far as we know,
It didn't. Yet there were no double takes,
No wrong turns such as *our* intelligence takes.
Seems as though Chemistry, allegorical figure
In robes the color of thought, had looked up, knowing
That the sampler she is here depicted as working
Called for a new molecular stitch. Where it takes

Root in her field—for the sampler, too, is a figure—
Buff canvas foothills, happy to be worked,
Turn green and gold, each morning's taller figures
Put forth leaves. Magic—and how it works
I begin to see. There've been hours, alone at work,
Or with you last spring, watching the clabber of rapids
Under the bridge reanimate, refigure
The inert shadows we cast, when I felt my side
Pierced by her needle, and knew that in the works

Were disciplines to be mastered proudly, rapidly,
And without fuss. Whether you are at my side
Or off shooting a film, or tigers, or rapids,
Gemlike projects keep forming deep inside
Our mine. Under what pressures? Today's nine-sided
Figure, prismatic epitome, may at a turn

Of the kaleidoscope—nightfall is rapid
In these parts—yield to a fly's faceted vision
Hatching a micromorgue of suicides

From one poor sleeper. Buzzed awake, he turns
The light on—ah, how old! Who could have envisioned
Twenty years' loneliness, ill health, wrong turnings?
He opens a book, squinting to clear his vision:
"Against such dark views, Nature's best provision
Remains the tendency of certain organisms
Long on the verge of extinction to return
At depths or altitudes they had once been unfitted
To endure . . ." Eyes shut in all but visionary

Consent, he lets the words reorganize
Everything he lives for, until it all fits
Or until he forgets them. What's the inorganic
Teardrop in Bulgari's window to *these* fits
And flashes of blankness? But after just three fittings
Our black suits were ready. Quietly becoming,
Worn forth at midnight into the Piazza's organ-
Grinding hilarity, they offset the scene
Without exposing it as counterfeit.

Not that it was—confetti thick as the coming
Snow, lanterns, mock dirges—merely that this scene's
Flats and floats trundled out over the years had come
To seem less touching. Where we stood a throng obscenely
Masked went dancing through us. Us the unseen
Ghostly headsmen of their Hallowtide?
Now only was it dawning. Harsher lives would come,
Not of necessity human. Meanwhile our natures
Slept in Earth, awaiting the unforeseen.

Solutions whereby molecules are untied
Ribbonwise, or (to quote the technician) "denatured,"
Enervate the long lank threads of polypeptide.
Their one hope then's the prompt recall to nature,

To postures even of some preternatural
Kinkiness, as in yoga. Or like our lovers' knot.
Looming through psychic azure—woe betide
Its severer!—it also, if we concentrate,
One dawn will glitter from a further peak. In nature,

To reach the pass, you must follow, like it or not,
Trails of loam and caustic. By concentrating
On flamework overhead, ice to sun slipknotted,
Each climber sweats his own salt concentrate
Of courage. Innumerable, faster-stabbing traits
Reorient themselves within the substance
He has contracted to become. So let us not
Act like children. These are the Alps. High time
For the next deep breath. My hand. Hold. Concentrate.

Room set at infrared,
Mind at ultraviolet,
Organisms ever stranger,
Hallucinated on the slide, fluoresce:

Chains of gold tinsel, baubles of green fire
For the arterial branches—
Here at *Microcosmics Illustrated,* why,
Christmas goes on all year!

Defenseless, the patrician cells await
Invasion by barbaric viruses,
Another sack of Rome.
A new age. Everything we dread.

Dread? It crows for joy in the manger.
Joy? The tree sparkles on which it will die.

TONY: ENDING THE LIFE

Let's die like Romans,
Since we have lived like Grecians. VOLPONE

Across the sea at Alexandria,
Shallow and glittering, a single shroud-
Shaped cloud had stolen, leaving as it paused
The underworld dilated, a wide pupil's
Downward shaft. The not-yet-to-be mined
Villa, a fortune of stone cards each summer
Less readable, more crushing, lay in wait
Beneath the blue-green sand of the sea floor.
Plump in schoolboy shorts, you peered and peered.
For wasn't youth like that—its deep charades
Revealed to us alone by passing shades?
But then years, too, would pass. And in the glow
Of what came next, the Alexandria
You brought to life would up and go:
Bars, beaches, British troops (so slim—yum yum!),
The parties above all. Contagious laughter,
Sparkle and hum and flow,
Saved you from weighty insights just below;
Till from another shore
(Folégandros, the western end of Crete)
Age, astonished, saw those heavy things
Lifted by tricky prisms into light,
Lifted like holy offerings,
Gemlike, disinterested,
Within the fleet
Reliquary of wave upon wave as it crested.

*

One year in Athens I let my beard grow.
The locals took it for a badge of grief.
Had someone died? Not yet, I tried to joke.
Of course beards came in every conceivable format—
Dapper, avuncular, deadbeat . . .

Mine warned of something creepier—uh-oh!
For over throat and lips had spread a doormat
On which to wipe filth brought in from the street.

Unfair! The boys were talkative and fun;
Far cleaner than my mind, after a bath.
Such episodes, when all was said and done,
Sweetened their reflective aftermath:
The denizens discovered in a dive
Relieved us (if not long or overmuch).
"Just see," the mirror breathed, "see who's alive,
Who hasn't forfeited the common touch,

The longing to lead everybody's life"
—Lifelong daydream of precisely those
Whom privilege or talent set apart:
How to atone for the achieved uniqueness?
By dying everybody's death, dear heart—
Saint, terrorist, fishwife. Stench that appals.
Famines, machine guns, the Great Plague (your sickness),
Rending of garments, cries, mass burials.

I'd watched my beard sprout in the mirror's grave.
Mirrors *are* graves, as all can see:
Knew this emerging mask would outlast me,
Just as the life outlasts us, that we led . . .
And then one evening, off it came. No more
Visions of the deep. These lines behave
As if we were already gone—not so!
Although of course each time's a closer shave.

One New Year's Eve, on midnight's razor stroke,
Kisses, a round of whiskies. You then drew
Forth from your pocket a brightness, that season's new
Two drachma piece, I fancied, taking the joke
—But no. Proud of your gift, you warned: "Don't leave
The barman this. Look twice." My double take

Lit on a grave young fourteen-carat queen
In profile. Heavens preserve us! and long live

Orbits of Majesty whereby her solar
Metal sets the standard. (A certain five-dollar
Piece, redeemed for paper—astute maneuver—
Taught me from then on: don't trust Presidents.)
Here it buys real estate. From the packed bus's
Racket and reek a newly-struck face glints
No increment of doubt or fear debases.
Speaking of heavens, Maria, a prime mover

In ours, one winter twilight telephoned:
Not for you to see her so far gone,
But to pick up, inside the unlatched door,
A satchel for safe keeping. *Done and done,*
You called from home to say. But such a weight,
Who lifted it? No one. She'd had to kick,
Inch by inch, your legacy down the hall,
The heavy bag of gold, her setting sun.

*

The sea is dark here at day's end
And the moon gaunt, half-dead
Like an old woman—like Madame Curie
Above her vats of pitchblende
Stirred dawn to dusk religiously
Out in the freezing garden shed.

It is a boot camp large and stark
To which you will be going.
Wave upon wave of you. The halls are crowded,
Unlit, the ceiling fixtures shrouded.
Advancing through the crush, the matriarch
Holds something up, mysteriously glowing.

Fruit of her dream and labor, see, it's here
(See too how scarred her fingertips):
The elemental sliver
Of matter heading for its own eclipse
And ours—this "lumière de l'avenir"
Passed hand to hand with a faint shiver:

Light that confutes the noonday blaze.
A cool uncanny blue streams from her vial,
Bathing the disappearers
Who asked no better than to gaze and gaze . . .
Too soon your own turn came. Denial
No longer fogged the mirrors.

You stumbled forth into the glare—
Blood-red ribbon where you'd struck your face.
Pills washed down with ouzo hadn't worked.
Now while the whole street buzzed and lurked
The paramedics left you there,
Returning costumed for a walk in Space.

The nurse thrust forms at you to sign,
Then flung away her tainted pen.
. . . . Lie back now in that heat
Older than Time, whose golden regimen
Still makes the palm grow tall and the date sweet . . .
Come, a last sip of wine.

Lie back. Over the sea
Sweeps, faint at first, the harpist's chord.
Purple with mourning, the royal barge gasps nearer.
Is it a test? a triumph? No more terror:
How did your namesake, lovesick Antony,
Meet the end? By falling on his sword

—A story in Plutarch
The plump boy knew from History class.
Slowly the room grows dark.
Stavro who's been reading you the news
Turns on a nightlight. No more views.
Just your head, nodding off in window-glass.

b o d y

Look closely at the letters. Can you see,
entering (stage right), then floating full,
then heading off—so soon—
how like a little kohl-rimmed moon
o plots her course from *b* to *d*

—as *y*, unanswered, knocks at the stage door?
Looked at too long, words fail,
phase out. Ask, now that *body* shines
no longer, by what light you learn these lines
and what the *b* and *d* stood for.

III

PLEDGE

House on alert.
Sun setting in a blaze
Of insight kisses book and budvase
Where they hurt.

Did the page-turner yawn and slacken,
Or an omen flip by unread?
Prime cuts that once bled
Now blacken.

Her brimming eyes say
More than they see.
He is all worried probity
About to get its way.

Dance steps the world knows curiously well
Ease them asunder—
Friends "rallying round her,"
His "move to a hotel."

Which one will get
The finger-wagging metronome,
Which one make a home
For the agèd cricket

Who sang togetherness ahead
From a hearth glowing bright?
It's dark now. I write
Propped up in bed:

"You who have drained dry
Your golden goblet are about to learn—
As in my turn
Have I—

Pledge

How life, unsweetened, fizzing up again
Fills the heart.
I drink to you apart
In that champagne."

COSMO

*People who love animals
once loved people.*   HOWARD MOSS

I

Because you are a terrier
—"earth-dog," a digger—
it's only natural, once on the bed,
you'll burrow fast and far as you can
between the strata of percale
dark geometric green/black/red
and in the heat of *our* four feet
frantically storm the badger's "hole"—
one of the many in your head.
What's going on here—instinct? art?
The cave, by all your faith undeepened,
is worried wide awake, a lover's heart.

2

You have some funny genes. Your grandfather
is known as One-Take Toby. There he stands
in the latest *Life:* on his hind legs, tongue-happy,
spangled tutu, Hedda Hopper hat.
Noticing your interest in our closets,
we exchange the eyes-to-heaven look of parents.
We want you to grow up to be All Dog,
the way they wanted me All Boy. My mother at least
seems reconciled. Last week when your "other Daddy"
manhandled you, planted kisses on your belly,
she laughed, "If there's a life after this one,
I wouldn't mind coming back as Peter's next dog."

3

Alpha males? That's what your other
Daddy and I must practise being—
to which end we wrestle your Feistiness
onto its back (lucky you're still a puppy).

69

The hand of the cradling arm clasps your hind feet,
my right hand lightly steadying your jaw.
Now a mesmeric "gaze of dominance"
initiates convulsions. Whimperings.
Two or three mortifying yawns.
Eyes rolling like an oracle's, Ego fades
into the submissive trance . . .
There! You learn quickly. It took me decades.

4
Housebroken (almost) and street-wise
—if wise is the word for those ecstatic
genital explorations, that intent
snuffling-up of germs four gleaming hypodermic
angels guard you from—you are rehearsing
in microcosm years I hardly remember,
being three hundred times your twelve weeks old.
You're gaining on me steadily, but still:
each time a new dog thrills you, the excitement—
(What *is* that in your mouth—a frozen turd?. . .
And what's that flutter in your nerves—a bird!)
Yes, yes, it comes back. With a difference.

5
Daddies also have their differences,
smelt out by you in the first hour; by us
only this tenth year faced as terminal.
So parting lies ahead—oh, not this month
with snow whipping and howling round the block,
but "in the season of flowers" (*La Bohème*).
And you? You'll go with him. He'll go
to his recuperation, I to mine;
not that a simple "Heal!" is all it takes.
When (if) I go to visit, there you'll be,
our Inner Dog, in perfect loyalty
. . . to whom? Is this how it was meant to be?

6

(Next summer, when the visit comes to pass,
Surprise: the neighbor's big fat iron-gray mammy
at tether's end. Like one of my formative loves,
she yearns to take that white child on her lap
and teach him the songs of slavery. . . . Then, the cat:
both of you at it—bark, hiss, chase—all day
like Hepburn and Tracy in a 40s movie
or scenes from the love going on above your head
ever since you can remember. Well. Time to plant
what but a bed of cosmos by the fence,
then lick your master's hands goodbye—just kidding—
and leave you in them. Meanwhile—) Winter still:

7

three gelid souls in the city. P at a runthrough,
me tired by errands. Heading back to bed,
I pass you open-eyed deep in your bed
on the toy-littered pantry floor,
jaw propped upon a ledge of faux sheepskin . . .
I lay myself down deep and open-eyed
lonely upon the ramparts of goosedown—
doing what? Experiencing Repose.
Each in the same position, the same mood.
Cold, shutter-filtered sun. A lassitude
learned from you by me? by me from you?
Nothing to think of or look forward to.

Timelessness passing. Man and his best friend.

RADIO

Behind grillwork (buff plastic
In would-be deco style)
The war goes on. With each further
Hair's-breadth turn of the dial:
"Kids love it—" "Sex probe in Congress
Triggers rage and denial,"

The weatherman predicting
Continued cold and rain,
Then high-frequency wails of
All too human pain.
Announcer: "That was a test. Now
'Nights in the Gardens of Spain'."

A black man's mild, exhausted
"Honey, I could be wrong . . ."
Gives rise to snickers of static
—But wait. Listen. This long
Ghastly morning, one station
Has never stopped playing our song.

FAMILY WEEK AT ORACLE RANCH

1 *The Brochure*

The world outstrips us. In my day,
Had such a place existed,
It would have been advertised with photographs
Of doctors—silver hair, pince-nez—

Above detailed credentials,
Not this wide-angle moonscape, lawns and pool,
Patients sharing pain like fudge from home—
As if these were the essentials,

As if a month at what it invites us to think
Is little more than a fat farm for Anorexics,
Substance Abusers, Love & Relationship Addicts
Could help *you*, light of my life, when even your shrink . . .

The message, then? That costly folderol,
Underwear made to order in Vienna,
Who needs it! Let the soul hang out
At Benetton—stone-washed, one size fits all.

2 *Instead of Complexes*

Simplicities. Just seven words—AFRAID,
HURT, LONELY, etc.—to say it with.
Shades of the first watercolor box
(I "felt blue," I "saw red").

Also some tips on brushwork. Not to say
"Your silence hurt me,"
Rather, "When you said nothing I felt hurt."
No blame, that way.

Dysfunctionals like us fail to distinguish
Between the two modes at first.
While the connoisseur of feeling throws up his hands:
Used to depicting personal anguish

With a full palette—hues, oils, glazes, thinner—
He stares into these withered wells and feels,
Well . . . SAD and ANGRY? Future lavender!
An infant Monet blinks beneath his skin.

3   *The Counsellors*

They're in recovery, too, and tell us from what,
And that's as far as it goes.
Like the sun-priests' in *The Magic Flute*
Their ritualized responses serve the plot.

Ken, for example, blond brows knitted: "When
James told the group he worried about dying
Without his lover beside him, I felt SAD."
Thank you for sharing, Ken,

I keep from saying; it would come out snide.
Better to view them as deadpan panels
Storing up sunlight for the woebegone,
Prompting from us lines electrified

By buried switches flipped (after how long!) . . .
But speak in private meanwhile? We may not
Until a voice within the temple lifts
Bans yet unfathomed into song.

4   *Gestalt*

Little Aileen is a gray plush bear
With button eyes and nose.
Perky in flowered smock and clean white collar,
She occupies the chair

Across from middleaged Big Aileen, face hid
In hands and hands on knees.
Her sobs break. In great waves it's coming back.
The uncle. What he did.

Little Aileen is her Inner Child
Who didn't . . . who didn't deserve. . . .
The horror kissed asleep, round Big Aileen
Fairytale thorns grow wild.

SADNESS and GUILT entitle us to watch
The survivor compose herself,
Smoothing the flowered stuff, which has ridden up,
Over an innocent gray crotch.

5   *Effects of Early "Religious Abuse"*

The great recurrent "sinner" found
In Dostoevsky—twisted mouth,
Stormlit eyes—before whose irresistible
Unworthiness the pure in heart bow down . . .

Cockcrow. Back across the frozen Neva
To samovar and warm, untubercular bed,
Far from the dens of vodka, mucus and semen,
They dream. I woke, the fever

Family Week at Oracle Ranch

Dripping insight, a spring thaw.
You and the others, wrestling with your demons,
Christs of self-hatred, Livingstones of pain,
Had drawn the lightning. In a flash I saw

My future: medic at some Armageddon
Neither side wins. I burned with SHAME for the years
You'd spent among sufferings uncharted—
Not even my barren love to rest your head on.

6   *The Panic*

Except that Oracle has maps
Of all those badlands. Just now, when you lashed out,
"There's a lot of disease in this room!"
And we felt our faith in one another lapse,

Ken had us break the circle and repair
To "a safe place in the room." Faster than fish
We scattered—Randy ducking as from a sniper,
Aileen, wedged in a corner, cradling her bear.

You and I stood flanking the blackboard,
Words as usual between us,
But backs to the same wall, for solidarity.
This magical sureness of movement no doubt scored

Points for all concerned, yet the only
Child each had become trembled for you
Thundering forth into the corridors,
Decibels measuring how HURT, how LONELY—

7   *Tunnel Vision*

New Age music. "Close your eyes now. You
Are standing," says the lecturer on Grief,
"At a tunnel's mouth. There's light at the end.
The walls, as you walk through

Are hung with images: who you loved that year,
An island holiday, a highschool friend.
Younger and younger, step by step—
And suddenly you're here,

At home. Go in. It's your whole life ago."
A pink eye-level sun flows through the hall.
"Smell the smells. It's supper time.
Go to the table." Years have begun to flow

Unhindered down my face. Why?
Because nobody's there. The grown-ups? Shadows.
The meal? A mirror. Reflect upon it. Before
Reentering the tunnel say goodbye,

8   *Time Recaptured*

Goodbye to childhood, that unhappy haven.
It's over, weep your fill. Let go
Of the dead dog, the lost toy. Practise grieving
At funerals—anybody's. Let go even

Of those first ninety seconds missed,
Fifty-three years ago, of a third-rate opera
Never revived since then. The GUILT you felt,
Adding it all the same to your master list!

Family Week at Oracle Ranch

Which is why, this last morning, when I switch
The FM on, halfway to Oracle,
And hear the announcer say
(Invisibly reweaving the dropped stitch),

"We bring you now the Overture
To Ambroise Thomas's seldom-heard *Mignon*,"
Joy (word rusty with disuse)
Flashes up, deserved and pure.

9   *Leading the Blind*

Is this you—smiling helplessly? Pinned to your chest,
A sign: *Confront Me if I Take Control.*
Plus you must wear (till sundown) a black eyeshade.
All day you've been the littlest, the clumsiest.

We're seated face to face. Take off your mask,
Ken says. Now look into each other deeply. Speak,
As far as you can trust, the words of healing.
Your pardon for my own blindness I ask;

You mine, for all you hid from me. Two old
Crackpot hearts once more aswim with color,
Our Higher Power has but to dip his brush—
Lo and behold!

The group approves. The ban lifts. Let me guide you,
Helpless but voluble, into a dripping music.
The rainbow brightens with each step. Go on,
Take a peek. This once, no one will chide you.

10   *The Desert Museum*

—Or, as the fat, nearsighted kid ahead
Construes his ticket, "Wow, Dessert Museum!"
I leave tomorrow, so you get a pass.
Safer, both feel, instead

Of checking into the No-Tell Motel,
To check it out—our brave new dried-out world.
Exhibits: crystals that for eons glinted
Before the wits did; fossil shells

From when this overlook lay safely drowned;
Whole spiny families repelled by sex,
Whom dying men have drunk from (Randy, frightened,
Hugging Little Randy, a red hound). . . .

At length behind a wall of glass, in shade,
The mountain lioness too indolent
To train them upon us unlids her gems
Set in the saddest face Love ever made.

11   *The Twofold Message*

(a) You are a brave and special person. (b)
There are far too many people in the world
For this to still matter for very long.
But (Ken goes on) since you obviously

Made the effort to attend Family Week,
We hope that we have shown you just how much
You have in common with everybody else.
Not to be "terminally unique"

Will be the consolation you take home.
Remember, Oracle is only the first step
In your recovery. The rest is up to you
And the twelve-step program you become

Involved in. An amazing forty per cent
Of our graduates are still clean after two years.
The rest? Well. . . . Given our society,
Sobriety is hard to implement.

12   *And If*

And if it were all like the moon?
Full this evening, bewitchingly
Glowing in a dark not yet complete
Above the world, explicit rune

Of change. Change is the "feeling" that dilutes
Those seven others to uncertain washes
Of soot and silver, inks unknown in my kit.
Change sends out shoots

Of FEAR and LONELINESS; of GUILT, as well,
Towards the old, abandoned patterns;
Of joy eventually, and self-forgiveness—
Colors few of us brought to Oracle . . .

And if the old patterns recur?
Ask how the co-dependent moon, another night,
Feels when the light drains wholly from her face.
Ask what that cold comfort means to her.

164 EAST 72ND STREET

These city apartment windows—my grandmother's once—
Must be replaced come Fall at great expense.
Pre-war sun shone through them on many a Saturday
Lunch unconsumed while frantic adolescence
Wheedled an old lady into hat and lipstick,
Into her mink, the taxi, the packed lobby,
Into our seats. Whereupon gold curtains parted
On Lakmé's silvery, not yet broken-hearted

Version of things as they were. But what remains
Exactly as it was except those panes?
Today's memo from the Tenants' Committee deplores
Even the ongoing deterioration
Of the *widows* in our building. Well. On the bright side,
Heating costs and street noise will be cut.
Sirens at present like intergalactic gay
Bars in full swing whoop past us night and day.

Sometimes, shocked wide awake, I've tried to reckon
How many lives—fifty, a hundred thousand?—
Are being shortened by that din of crosstown
Ruby flares, wherever blinds don't quite . . .
And shortened by how much? Ten minutes each?
Reaching the Emergency Room alive, the victim
Would still have to live *years,* just to repair
The sonic fallout of a single scare.

"Do you ever wonder where you'll—" Oh my dear,
Asleep somewhere, or at the wheel. Not here.
Within months of the bathroom ceiling's cave-in,
Which missed my grandmother by a white hair,
She moved back South. The point's to live in style,
Not to drop dead in it. On a carpet of flowers
Nine levels above ground, like Purgatory,
Our life is turning into a whole new story:

Juices, blue cornbread, afternoons at the gym—
Imagine who remembers how to swim!
Evenings of study, or intensive care
For one another. Early to bed. And later,
If the mirror's drowsy eye perceives a slight
But brilliant altercation between curtains
Healed by the leaden hand of—one of us?
A white-haired ghost? or the homunculus

A gentle alchemist behind them trains
To put in order these nocturnal scenes—
Two heads already featureless in gloom
Have fallen back to sleep. Tomorrow finds me
Contentedly playing peekaboo with a sylphlike
Quirk in the old glass, making the brickwork
On the street's far (bright) side ripple. Childhood's view.
My grandmother—an easy-to-see-through

Widow by the time she died—made it my own.
Bless her good sense. Far from those parts of town
Given to high finance, or the smash hit and steak house,
Macy's or crack, Saks or quick sex, this neighborhood
Saunters blandly forth, adjusting its clothing.
Things done in purple light before we met,
Uncultured things that twitched as on a slide
If thought about, fade like dreams. Two Upper East Side

Boys again! Rereading Sir Walter Scott
Or *Through the Looking Glass*, it's impossible not
To feel how adult life, with its storms and follies,
Is letting up, leaving me ten years old,
Trustful, inventive, once more good as gold
—And counting on this to help, should a new spasm
Wake the gray sleeper, or to improve his chances
When ceilings flush with unheard ambulances.

QUATRAINS FOR PEGASUS

Breakfast over, to Memorial Park we'd go
On sunny Saturdays, I and Nanny McGrath.
We took care to approach the monument each time
By a new swamp oak- or palmetto-shaded path.

The paths converged at the heart of a parched fairway
Where Earth, not looking her best, rose out of the blue
Reflecting pool: Earth starved to a global ribcage,
Meridians of bronze the empty sky glared through.

Yet round it four horses of stone still fairly white
(Or just the one horse times four—with reflections, eight)
Held up the globe in a caracole that thrilled me,
Eager like them for the further, the ultimate

Thrill due on the stroke of nine. A black man in rags—
Making no secret of it as we looked his way—
Grasped something below ground level and gave it a turn.
The circulatory system brought into play

Filled the air with a magical diamond surf
Hoofs came plunging through, jets like fireworks rocketed
In four directions, as though from the horses' brows.
I wondered if passing through a white horse's head

Was curing the municipal water for good
Of its butts and tinfoil? Making trees toss with joy,
Flagstones glitter and steam? Would the process also
Help Nanny's bad hip, make me a good boy,

And keep—for each morning paper brought fresh horrors—
Our whole world from starving like the Armenians,
Its bones from coming to light like the Lindberg baby's . . . ?
Nanny McGrath's young brother lay buried in France,

And these were questions—what if she knew the answers?—
I was too little and tactful to ask my nurse.
The more she said, the wickeder the world got.
Don't let it, I begged the horses, get any worse.

THE PYROXENES

Well, life has touched me, too.
No longer infant jade,
What is the soul not made
To drink in, to go through

As it becomes a self!
Admire this forest scene,
Dendritic, evergreen,
On Leto's back-lit shelf—

"Forest" that long predates
The kingdom of the trees.
Move on a step to these
Translucent spinach plates

Morbidly thin, which flake
On flake corundum-red
As weeping eyes embed.
You'd think poorhouse and wake,

Fury, bereavement, grief
Dwelt at Creation's core,
Maternal protoplast,
Millions of years before

Coming to high relief
Among us city folk.
Out of her woods at last,
On the Third Day we woke

From cradles deep in mire
At white heat: elements-
To-be of hard, scarred sense,
Strangers to fire.

PEARL

        Well, I admit
A small boy's eyes grew rounder and lips moister
To find it invisibly chained, at home in the hollow
Of his mother's throat: the real, deepwater thing.
    Far from the mind at six to plumb
X-raywise those glimmering lamplit
Asymmetries to self-immolating mite
        Or angry grain of sand
Not yet proverbial. Yet his would be the hand
        Mottled with survival—
    She having slipped (how? when?) past reach—
    That one day grasped it. Sign of what
But wisdom's trophy. Time to mediate,
Skin upon skin, so cunningly they accrete,
    The input. For its early mote
            Of grit
    Reborn as orient moon to gloat
In verdict over the shucked, outsmarted meat. . . .
One layer, so to speak, of calcium carbonate
    That formed in me is the last shot
    —I took the seminar I teach
        In Loss to a revival—
Of Sasha Guitry's classic *Perles de la Couronne.*
        The hero has tracked down
His prize. He's holding forth, that summer night,
At the ship's rail, all suavity and wit,
    Gem swaying like a pendulum
From his fing—oops! To soft bubble-blurred harpstring
Arpeggios regaining depths (man the camera, follow)
Where an unconscious world, my yawning oyster,
        Shuts on it.

OVERDUE PILGRIMAGE
TO NOVA SCOTIA

Elizabeth Bishop (1911–1979)

Your village touched us by not knowing how.
Even as we outdrove its clear stormlight
A shower of self-belittling brilliants fell.
Miles later, hours away, here are rooms full
Of things you would have known: pump organ, hymnal,
Small-as-life desks, old farm tools, charter, deed,
Schoolbooks (Greek Grammar, *A Canadian Reader*),
Queen Mary in oleograph, a whole wall hung
With women's black straw hats, some rather smart
—All circa 1915, like the manners
Of the fair, soft-spoken girl who shows us through.
Although till now she hasn't heard of you
She knows these things you would have known by heart
And we, by knowing you by heart, foreknew.

The child whose mother had been put away
Might wake, climb to a window, feel the bay
Steel itself, bosom bared to the full moon,
Against the woebegone, cerebral Man;
Or by judicious squinting make noon's red
Monarch grappling foreground goldenrod
Seem to extract a further essence from
Houses it dwarfed. Grown-up, the visitor
Could find her North by the green velvet map
Appliqued upon this wharfside shack,
Its shingles (in the time her back was turned)
Silver-stitched to visionary grain
As by a tireless, deeply troubled inmate,
Were Nature not by definition sane.

In living as in poetry, your art
Refused to tip the scale of being human
By adding unearned weight. "New, tender, quick"—
Nice watchwords; yet how often they invited
The anguish coming only now to light
In letters like photographs from Space, revealing
Your planet tremulously bright through veils
As swept, in fact, by inconceivable
Heat and turbulence—but there, I've done it,
Added the weight. What tribute could you bear
Without dismay? Well, facing where you lived
Somebody's been inspired (*can* he have read
"Filling Station"?) to put pumps, a sign:
ESSO—what else! We filled up at the shrine.

Look, those were elms! Long vanished from *our* world.
Elms, by whose goblet stems distance itself
Taken between two fingers could be twirled,
Its bouquet breathed. The trees looked cumbersome,
Sickly through mist, like old things on a shelf—
Astrolabes, pterodactyls. They must know.
The forest knows. Out from such melting backdrops
It's the rare conifer stands whole, one sharp
Uniquely tufted spoke of a dark snow crystal
Not breathed upon, as yet, by our exhaust.
Part of a scene that with its views and warblers,
And at its own grave pace, but in your footsteps
—Never more imminent the brink, more sheer—
Is making up its mind to disappear

. . . With many a dirty look. That waterfall
For instance, beating itself to grit-veined cream
"Like Roquefort through a grater"? Or the car—!
So here we sit in the car-wash, snug and dry
As the pent-up fury of the storm hits: streaming,
Foaming "emotions"—impersonal, cathartic,
Closer to both art and what we are
Than the gush of nothings one outpours to people
On the correspondence side of bay and steeple
Whose dazzling whites we'll never see again,
Or failed to see in the first place. Still, as the last
Suds glide, slow protozoa, down the pane,
We're off—Excuse our dust! With warm regards,—
Gathering phrases for tomorrow's cards.

ALESSIO AND THE ZINNIAS

One summer—was he eight?—
They gave him a seed packet
Along with a 2′ by 4′
Slice of the estate.

To grow, to grow, grim law
Without appeal!
He, after all, kept growing every day . . .
Now this redundant chore.

Up sprouted green enough
For the whole canton, had one known to thin it.
Michaelmas found him eye to eye
With a gang of ruffians

Not askable indoors,
Whose gaudy, rigid attitudes
("Like pine cones in drag")
There was scant question of endorsing

—Much as our droll friend, their legatee,
Would reap from them over the years. For instance:
Think twice before causing
Just anything to be.

Then: *Hold your head high in the stinking*
Throngs of kind.
Joyously assimilate the Sun.
Never wear orange or pink.

SELF-PORTRAIT IN TYVEK (TM) WINDBREAKER

The windbreaker is white with a world map.
DuPont contributed the seeming-frail,
Unrippable stuff first used for Priority Mail.
Weightless as shores reflected in deep water,
The countries are violet, orange, yellow, green;
Names of the principal towns and rivers, black.
A zipper's hiss, and the Atlantic Ocean closes
Over my blood-red T-shirt from the Gap.

I found it in one of those vaguely imbecile
Emporia catering to the collective unconscious
Of our time and place. This one featured crystals,
Cassettes of whalesong and rain-forest whistles,
Barometers, herbal cosmetics, pillows like puffins,
Recycled notebooks, mechanized lucite coffins
For sapphire waves that crest, break, and recede,
As they presumably do in nature still.

Sweat-panted and Reeboked, I wear it to the gym.
My terry-cloth headband is green as laurel.
A yellow plastic Walkman at my hip
Sends shiny yellow tendrils to either ear.
All us street people got our types on tape,
Turn ourselves on with a sly fingertip.
Today I felt like Songs of Yesteryear
Sung by Roberto Murolo. Heard of him?

Well, back before animal species began to become
Extinct, a dictator named Mussolini banned
The street-singers of Naples. One smart kid
Learned their repertoire by heart, and hid.
Emerging after the war with his guitar,
He alone bearing the old songs of the land
Into the nuclear age sang with a charm,
A perfect naturalness that thawed the numb

Survivors and reinspired the Underground.
From love to grief to gaiety his art
Modulates effortlessly, like a young man's heart,
Tonic to dominant—the frets so few
And change so strummed into the life of things
That Nature's lamps burn brighter when he sings
Nannetta's fickleness, or chocolate,
Snow on a flower, the moon, the seasons' round.

I picked his tape in lieu of something grosser
Or loftier, say the Dead or Arvo Pärt,
On the hazy premise that what fills the mind
Shows on the face. My face, as a small part
Of nature, hopes this musical sunscreen
Will keep the wilderness within it green,
Yet looks uneasy, drawn. I detect behind
My neighbor's grin the oncoming bulldozer

And cannot stop it. Ecosaints—their karma
To be Earth's latest, maybe terminal, fruits—
Are slow to ripen. Even this dumb jacket
Probably still believes in Human Rights,
Thinks in terms of "nations", urban centers,
Cares less (can Tyvek breathe?) for oxygen
Than for the innocents evicted when
Ford bites the dust and Big Mac buys the farm.

Hah. As if greed and savagery weren't the tongues
We've spoken since the beginning. My point is, those
Prior people, fresh from scarifying
Their young and feasting in triumph on their foes,
Honored the gods of Air and Land and Sea.
We, though . . . Cut to dead forests, filthy beaches,
The can of hairspray, oil-benighted creatures,
A star-scarred x-ray of the North Wind's lungs.

Still, not to paint a picture wholly black,
Some social highlights: Dead white males in malls.
Prayer breakfasts. Pay-phone sex. "Ring up as meat."
Oprah. The GNP. The contour sheet.
The painless death of History. The stick
Figures on Capitol Hill. Their rhetoric,
Gladly—no, rapturously (on Prozac) suffered!
Gay studies. Right to Lifers. The laugh track.

And clothes. Americans, blithe as the last straw,
Shrug off accountability by dressing
Younger than their kids—jeans, ski-pants, sneakers,
A baseball cap, a happy-face T-shirt . . .
Like first-graders we "love" our mother Earth,
Know she's been sick, and mean to care for her
When we grow up. Seeing my windbreaker,
People hail me with nostalgic awe.

"Great jacket!" strangers on streetcorners impart.
The Albanian doorman pats it: "Where you buy?"
Over his ear-splitting drill a hunky guy
Yells, "Hey, you'll always know where you are, right?"
"Ever the fashionable cosmopolite,"
Beams Ray. And "Voilà mon pays"—the carrot-haired
Girl in the bakery, touching with her finger
The little orange France above my heart.

Everyman, c'est moi, the whole world's pal!
The pity is how soon such feelings sour.
As I leave the gym a smiling-as-if-I-should-know-her
Teenager—oh but I *mean*, she's wearing "our"
Windbreaker, and assumes. . . . Yet I return her wave
Like an accomplice. For while all humans aren't
Countable as equals, we must behave
As if they were, or the spirit dies (Pascal).

Self-Portrait in Tyvek(TM) Windbreaker

"We"? A few hundred decades of relative
Lucidity glinted-through by minnow schools
Between us and the red genetic muck—
Everyman's underpainting. We look up, shy
Creatures, from our trembling pool of sky.
Caught wet-lipped in light's brushwork, fleet but sure,
Flash on shudder, folk of the first fuck,
Likeness breeds likeness, fights for breath—*I live*—

Where the crush thickens. And by season's end,
The swells of fashion cresting to collapse
In breaker upon breaker on the beach,
Who wants to be caught dead in this cliché
Of mere "involvement"? Time to put under wraps
Its corporate synthetic global pitch;
Not throwing out motley once reveled in,
Just learning to live down the wrinkled friend.

Face it, reproduction of any kind leaves us colder
Though airtight-warmer (greenhouse effect) each year.
Remember the figleaf's lesson. Styles betray
Some guilty knowledge. What to dress ours in—
A seer's blind gaze, an infant's tender skin?
All that's been seen through. The eloquence to come
Will be precisely what we cannot say
Until it parts the lips. But as one grows older

—I should confess before that last coat dries—
The wry recall of thunder does for rage.
Erotic torrents flash on screens instead
Of drenching us. Exclusively in dream,
These nights, does a grandsire rear his saurian head,
And childhood's inexhaustible brain-forest teem
With jewel-bright lives. No way now to restage
Their sacred pageant under our new skies'

Irradiated lucite. What then to wear
When—hush, it's no dream! It's my windbreaker
In black, with starry longitudes, Archer, Goat,
Clothing an earphoned archangel of Space,
Who hasn't read Pascal, and doesn't wave . . .
What far-out twitterings he learns by rote,
What looks they'd wake upon a human face,
Don't ask, Roberto. Sing our final air:

Love, grief etc. * * * * for good reason.
Now only * * * * * * * STOP signs.
Meanwhile * * * * * if you or I've ex-
ceeded our [?] * * * ~~more than time~~ was needed
To fit a text airless and * * as Tyvek
With breathing spaces and between the lines
Days brilliantly recurring, as once *we* did,
To keep the blue wave dancing in its prison.

AN UPWARD LOOK

O heart green acre   sown with salt
by the departing   occupier

lay down your gallant   spears of wheat
Salt of the earth   each stellar pinch

flung in blind   defiance backwards
now takes its toll   Up from his quieted

quarry the lover   colder and wiser
hauling himself   finds the world turning

toys triumphs   toxins into
this vast facility   the living come
dearest to die in   How did it happen

In bright alternation   minutely mirrored
within the thinking   of each and every

mortal creature   halves of a clue
approach the earthlights   Morning star

evening star   salt of the sky
First the grave   dissolving into dawn

then the crucial   recrystallizing
from inmost depths   of clear dark blue

A NOTE ABOUT THE AUTHOR

James Merrill was born in New York City on March 3, 1926, and lived in Stonington, Connecticut. He was the author of twelve books of poems, which won him two National Book Awards (for *Nights and Days* and *Mirabell*), the Bollingen Prize in Poetry (for *Braving the Elements*), the Pulitzer Prize (for *Divine Comedies*) and the first Bobbitt National Prize for Poetry awarded by the Library of Congress (for *The Inner Room*). *The Changing Light at Sandover* appeared in 1982 and included the long narrative poem begun with "The Book of Ephraim" (from *Divine Comedies*), plus *Mirabell: Books of Number* and *Scripts for the Pageant* in their entirety; it received the National Book Critics Circle Award in poetry for 1983. *Late Settings* appeared in 1985. In addition to the one volume edition of his narrative poem *The Changing Light at Sandover*, he also issued two selected volumes: *From the First Nine, Poems (1946–1976)* (1982), and *Selected Poems, 1946–1985* (1992). He was the author of two novels, *The (Diblos) Notebook* (1965, reissued in 1994) and *The Seraglio* (1957, reissued in 1987) and two plays, *The Immortal Husband* (first produced in 1955 and published in *Playbook* the following year), and, in one act, *The Bait*, published in *Artist's Theater* (1960). A book of essays, *Recitative*, appeared in 1986, and in 1993 a memoir, *A Different Person*. His last book of poems, *A Scattering of Salts*, was published in 1995, following his untimely death on February 6 of that year.

A NOTE ON THE TYPE

The text of this book was set in Plantin, a digitized verison of a type face cut in 1913 by The Monotype Corporation, London. Though the face bears the name of the great Christopher Plantin, who in the latter part of the sixteenth century owned, in Antwerp, the largest printing and publishing firm in Europe, it is a rather free adaptation of designs by Claude Garamond (c. 1480–1561) made for that firm. With its strong, simple lines, Plantin is a no-nonsense face of exceptional legibility.

Composition by Graphic Composition, Inc.,
Athens, Georgia
Printed and Bound by Quebecor Printing,
Kingsport, Tennessee
Designed by Harry Ford